EVERYDAY CODING__

INFORMATION AND ACTION

Using Variables

Derek Miller

Cavendish Square

New York

Published in 2018 by Cavendish Square Publishing, LLC
243 5th Avenue, Suite 136, New York, NY 10016

Copyright © 2018 by Cavendish Square Publishing, LLC

First Edition

Website: cavendishsq.com

Library of Congress Cataloging-in-Publication Data

Names: Miller, Derek L.
Title: Information and action: using variables / Derek L. Miller.
Description: New York : Cavendish Square, 2018. | Series: Everyday coding | Includes
bibliographical references and index. | Audience: Grades 2-6.
Identifiers: ISBN 9781502629975 (library bound) | ISBN 9781502629951 (pbk.)
| ISBN 9781502629968 (6 pack) | ISBN 9781502629982 (ebook)
Subjects: LCSH: Computer programming--Juvenile literature. | Variables (Mathematics)--Juvenile literature.
Classification: LCC QA76.52 M55 2018 | DDC 005.1--dc23

Editorial Director: David McNamara
Editor: Caitlyn Miller
Copy Editor: Nathan Heidelberger
Associate Art Director: Amy Greenan
Designer: Christina Shults
Production Coordinator: Karol Szymczuk
Photo Research: J8 Media

The photographs in this book are used by permission and through the courtesy of:

Photo credits: Cover Jonathan Kirn/The Image Bank/Getty Images; p. 4 Alexandra Grablewski/Digital Vision/
Getty Images; p. 8 Best-Backgrounds/Shutterstock.com; p. 9 K-S/Alamy Stock Photo; p. 10 Elena Abrazhevich/
Shutterstock.com; p. 11 Julie Alissi/J8 Media; p. 12 Monkeybusinessimages/iStockphoto.com; p. 14
Pavel Bobrovskiy/Shutterstock.com; p. 16 Jtairat/iStockphoto.com; p. 17 Photographee.eu/Shutterstock.
com; p. 18 (clockwise from top left) Lliveinoctober/Shutterstock.com, Billion Photos/Shutterstock.com,
Pongsakorn Chaina/Shutterstock.com; p. 18 Ducu59us/Shutterstock.com; p. 19 Phovoir/Alamy Stock Photo;
p. 20 RF_vector/Shutterstock.com; p. 21 OLJ Studio/Shutterstock.com; p. 22 Marc Bruxelle/Shutterstock.
com; p. 25 Hecho/Shutterstock.com; p. 26 Leslie Plaza Johnson/Icon Sportswire/Corbis/Getty Images.

Printed in the United States of America

TABLE OF CONTENTS __

Coding with Variables

What do you do when you need to remember something? You might repeat it over and over until you memorize it. Or you might write it down in a safe place. A homework planner is a good example.

A computer can't do either of these things. It has to use a **variable** to store information. Variables are like boxes that hold some

Opposite: Variables store information, just like your notebook does.

information. When a computer needs to look at or change information, it uses a variable. This is just like you looking at your homework planner.

Variables let computers do all sorts of cool things. Computers that chart a spaceship's course to the moon use variables. Video games remember your player name using variables. Let's look at some more examples of variables.

CHAPTER 01

A Closer Look at Variables

Variables are like people's names. We use a person's name when we want to talk about someone. We could say, "My friend who sits next to me in math class." But it's a lot easier to say "John."

When a **computer program** uses a piece of information over and over, it is usually a variable. This makes things a whole lot easier. A variable name is a short way to refer to information. It's like a person's name in everyday life.

```
}public List<List<Integer>> levelOrder(Call,
return null;}i.processData("{3,39,20,#,5,1#5
kimport java.util.*;import java.lang.*;impo
lass JavaProgram{public static void main (S
hrows java.lang.Exception{public static voi
 args){BufferedReader file_reader = new Bu
ew InputStreamReader (System.in));String t
ext=file_reader.readLine(file_contents)).e
ystem.out.println(text);int a;for (int i=
++;for (int j=0;x[j]!='\0';j++){z[a+j]=x[
Optimization{int val;Optimization left;Op
ight;public Optimization(int x) { val = x
                    D-+-(String words) {S
```

Programs are made up of code.

All variables have names. Good programmers make sure their variable names are simple. That way, anyone looking at the program **code** can figure out what a variable is. A computer code shouldn't be difficult to understand. It's not supposed to be a secret code. It should be clear and easy to follow. Good variable names keep things simple.

One variable you have probably seen in video games is your score. As you play, it goes up and down. The computer program stores your score as a variable. It then changes the **value** of the variable as you play.

This is a good example for the second thing that all variables have: a value. The value is the information that a variable stores. A variable only has one value.

Here, the score variable has a value of 18,000.

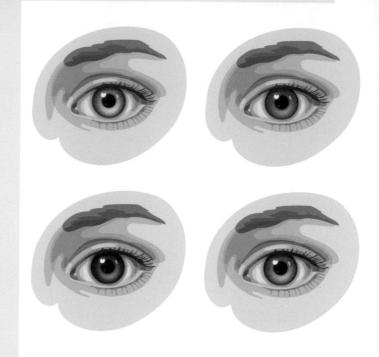

Variables can be colors and words as well as numbers.

Think It Over

The value of a variable doesn't have to be a number. Imagine a variable named "eye color." What would its value be for you? What about for your friends and family? Could the value of this variable change?

The number of blocks you have in *Minecraft* is stored as a variable.

When you play a game, you only have one score. It wouldn't make any sense if your score was two different numbers, like ten and fifteen.

Although a variable has just one value, the value can change over time (but it doesn't have to). This is one of the main reasons that computer programs use variables. Variables can be changed easily. You start the game at one score. As you play, the program changes your score. It

You can measure your height to see a real-life variable that changes over time.

remembers that piece of information. A variable is the easiest way for a program to do this.

Variables are very important for computers. But we can also see variables all around us. Look in the mirror. You can see something that changes all the time—how tall you are. Your height is a variable. It changes constantly. Last year, you were shorter than you are now. Next year, you'll be even taller.

If you were writing a computer program, you would probably name this variable "height." Then, the value of the variable would be how tall you are. The value would keep changing until you stopped growing. Then, it would stay the same. Yet the name would always be "height."

CHAPTER 02

Variables in Everyday Life

Can you think of something in everyday life with a name that holds information? Maybe you thought of a box or a drawer. These are a lot like variables. If you put a label on a box, that is like the variable name. What's inside the box is like the value.

Opposite: Variables are like labeled boxes that store information.

Think of a variable as a box or a drawer. But remember, a variable stores only one value!

There is one main difference between labeled boxes and variables. Boxes can have more than one thing inside of them. You could have a box with many different toys inside. That's not exactly like a variable because a variable only has one value.

Variables are often compared to envelopes. Imagine an envelope with a letter inside. It is labeled on the outside—maybe

Envelopes contain letters just as variables contain information.

with a friend's name. The letter inside is like the value. You can switch the letter out for a different one. Now it has a different value. The envelope stays the same, just like a variable with a changing value.

Now think of all the different things you can put inside an envelope. Perhaps you want to send someone a picture. Or perhaps you are playing a math game and need to put a number inside. Whatever you put in the envelope, it is still an envelope.

Variables can store words, images, numbers, or even the fact that something is true or false.

Variables are just like this, too. They can store different kinds of information. They can store numbers, words, colors, or even **images**. These are called **data types**. The data type of a variable is really important.

A math notebook stores numbers. A language arts notebook stores words.

Imagine your teacher tells you to take a picture out of a folder and color it in. But when you open the folder, it has a math worksheet in it. There's no picture to color! You can't do what your teacher said. You'd have to ask for help. Variables can have the same problem. If the variable has the wrong data type, it can cause all sorts of **bugs**. Programs can't ask for help. A bad variable can make a program stop working.

If a variable is a number, the computer can change it by adding or subtracting. But what if it's a color? A computer can't add twenty to a color data type. Trying to do this will make the program **crash**. Red plus twenty doesn't make any sense. This is why data type is so important. Variables can do different things based on their data type.

Variables need to be the right data type or errors occur.

The amount of money in your wallet or bank account is like a variable. It is a value that changes.

Inside Your Piggy Bank

What's a value that changes all the time in your life? Think about how much money you have right now. Is it the same as yesterday? How much money you have is like the value of a variable. It changes often. You get or spend money all the time.

CHAPTER 03

Bringing It All Together

Different people speak different languages. English and Spanish have different rules. You can say the same thing in both languages, though. The basic building blocks, like **nouns** and **verbs**, are used in all languages. Variables in computer **programming languages** are like nouns or verbs. They are so basic that we need to use them.

Opposite: Video games like *Pokémon Go* are programmed using variables.

Computer programs are written in many different programming languages. These different languages are written in different ways. Code written in one language might not work in another. But one similarity that many different languages have is variables. Even though they are written in different ways, they need variables to work. And variables always have a name and a value.

Variables can be used to make programs **interactive**. Have you ever played a game that asked you to pick a name? That program probably used a variable. The game stored the name you entered as the value of a variable. Then, it used the variable to repeat the name back to you. The game might have started with "Hi, (name)!" It had to use a variable to do this.

Usernames and passwords are often stored as variables.

It is variables that allow programs to be flexible and interactive. They let programs store information that a user enters. Variables also let programs change that information and use it in cool ways. This is what makes computers so powerful. They can store and change data to perform all sorts of tasks.

You will have to use variables when you learn how to code computer programs. You'll see firsthand just how important they are. Your program will probably need to store information no matter what it does. Variables make this easy. Remember, they need to be the right data

Some variables control the flow of a computer program the same way umpires control the flow of a baseball game.

You're Out!

Some variables can only have one of two values: true or false. These variables are called **Boolean variables**. They often control the flow of a program. They are similar to an umpire in a game of baseball shouting "out" or "safe" when a player slides into home. What the umpire says determines the flow of the game.

type. They also need a simple name. Using data types and picking good names are some of the first things you will learn as a coder. Don't forget them!

Programs of all kinds use variables to accomplish their goals. Whether it is a computer game or an important program like Microsoft Word, variables make it run. This might sound hard or confusing. It's actually simple. Just think back to how variables are containers.

You could be thinking of a folder or a bucket. These containers hold information just as variables do in programming. And computer programs need this information to respond to your actions. If you're having fun playing a game, you have variables to thank!

GLOSSARY

Boolean variables Variables with two values: true or false.

bugs Errors in a computer code.

code The instructions that make a computer program work.

computer program Instructions that allow a computer to do some task. For example, *Minecraft* and Microsoft Word are computer programs.

crash When a program crashes, it stops working.

data type The kind of information that a variable stores. Examples include numbers, words, and images.

image A picture on a screen.

interactive When a program is interactive, it responds to the user. The user can change what the program does.

nouns The part of speech that includes people, places, things, and names.

programming languages Different languages used to write computer programs. Each language has different rules.

value The information stored by a variable. It can be many things depending on the data type, such as a number, a picture, or words.

variable What a computer uses to store information. All variables have a name and a value.

verbs The part of speech for action words like "run."

Books

Lyons, Heather, and Elizabeth Tweedale.

Kids Get Coding: A World of Programming.

Minneapolis: Lerner Publishing, 2016.

Woodcock, John. *DK Workbooks: Computer Coding*.

New York: DK Publishing, 2014.

Websites

CS Principles: Intro to Variables—Part 1

https://www.youtube.com/watch?v=G41G_PEWFjE

Code.org explains what a variable is in a fun way.

How Do Computer Programs Use Variables?

http://www.bbc.co.uk/guides/zw3dwmn

The BBC introduces variables in this great guide.

INDEX __

Derek Miller is a teacher who writes about history and technology. He is the author of *Completing Tasks: Using Algorithms* and *Group Planning, Creating, and Testing: Programming Together*. Derek likes to play computer games. He's always trying to improve his score variable.